Arnold Plays Baseball

ABC Adventures

Written by Pat Whitehead

Illustrated by G. Brian Karas

Troll Associates

Library of Congress Cataloging in Publication Data

Whitehead, Patricia.
    Arnold plays baseball.

    (ABC adventures)
    Summary: Arnold is unhappy and restless when rainy
weather keeps him from playing his favorite game, base-
ball. A letter of the alphabet appears on each page
accompanied by an appropriate word from the text.
    1. Children's stories, American. [1. Baseball—
Fiction. 2. Dogs—Fiction. 3. Rain and rainfall—
Fiction. 4. Alphabet] I. Karas, G. Brian, ill.
II. Title. III. Series: Whitehead, Patricia.
ABC adventures.
PZ7.W5852Ar   1985   [E]   84-8827
ISBN 0-8167-0367-1 (lib. bdg.)
ISBN 0-8167-0368-X (pbk.)

Aa

angry

Meet Arnold. Arnold is angry.

Bb

baseball

Arnold wants to play baseball. Arnold's
mother says no—no baseball today.

Cc

cannot

"You cannot, Arnold. You cannot go
outside," says his mother. "It's raining."

Dd

day

Poor Arnold.
He would play baseball all day if he could.

Ee

every

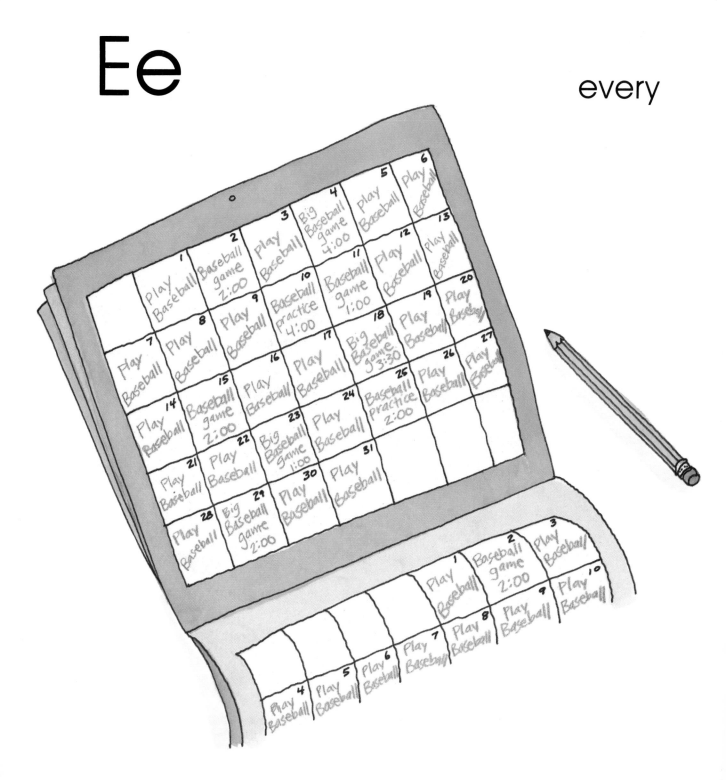

Arnold would play every day—if he could.

Ff

field

If the field is muddy, Arnold doesn't mind.

Gg

ground

If the ground is wet, Arnold doesn't care.

Hh

Home plate

Home plate is under a puddle.
"So what?" says Arnold.

Ii

indoors

Poor Arnold. He has to stay indoors.

Jj

jacket

He takes off his jacket.

Kk

kicks

He kicks off his shoes.

LI

leaves

He leaves his bat by the door.

Mm

mitt

And he puts his mitt away.

Nn

Now

Now what? Now what can he do?

Oo

ought

There ought to be something to do indoors.

Pp

plays

Arnold plays his drums.

Qq

Quiet

Quiet, Arnold. Be quiet.

Rr

runs

Arnold runs through the house.

Stop, Arnold. Stop running.

Tt

trips

Arnold trips. Arnold trips and falls.

Uu

upset

Poor Arnold. He is upset. His mother is upset.

Vv

very

Just then it is very quiet.

Ww

window

Arnold runs to the window.

Xx

exclaims

"It stopped! The rain has stopped,"
exclaims Arnold.

Yy

yells

"Yippee," yells Arnold. "Yippee," yells Arnold's mother.

Zz

Zip

"Zip up your jacket, Arnold," says his
mother. "It's wet outside." Zip, zip.

Arnold doesn't mind. He's off to play baseball.

Lucky Arnold!